SWALLOWED LIGHT

SWALLOWED LIGHT
MICHAEL WASSON

COPPER CANYON PRESS

PORT TOWNSEND, WASHINGTON

Cover art: Anne Rearick, *Filleting the Salmon, Lapwai, Idaho,* 2010

Copper Canyon Press is in residence at Fort Worden State Park in Port Townsend, Washington, under the auspices of Centrum. Centrum is a gathering place for artists and creative thinkers from around the world, students of all ages and backgrounds, and audiences seeking extraordinary cultural enrichment.

LIBRARY OF CONGRESS CATALOGING-IN-PUBLICATION DATA

Names: Wasson, Michael, author.
Title: Swallowed light / Michael Wasson.
Description: Port Townsend, Washington : Copper Canyon Press, [2022] |
    Summary: "Collection of poems by Michael Wasson"— Provided by
    publisher.
Identifiers: LCCN 2021053286 (print) | LCCN 2021053287 (ebook) |
ISBN 9781556596001 (paperback) | ISBN 9781619322530 (epub)
Subjects: LCGFT: Poetry.
Classification: LCC PS3623.A86826 S93 2022 (print) |
LCC PS3623.A86826 (ebook) | DDC 811/.6—dc23
LC record available at https://lccn.loc.gov/2021053286
LC ebook record available at https://lccn.loc.gov/2021053287

9 8 7 6 5 4 3 2 first printing

COPPER CANYON PRESS

Post Office Box 271
Port Townsend, Washington 98368
www.coppercanyonpress.org

ACKNOWLEDGMENTS

Earlier versions of poems in this book appeared in the following publications:

American Poets: "The Exile"

Beloit Poetry Journal: "Ezekiel 37:3," "Self-Portrait as Article 1[1]. [Treaty with the Nez Percés, 1855]: Cession of Lands to the United States"

Blood Orange Review: "I Say After-Rain, You Say *hahalxpáawisa*," "Objects in Mirror Are Closer Than They Appear," "Years Later, *na'pláx,* in the Yard, Asks Me to Rename Him"

Broadsided Press: "Close to Each Other with [a/the] Body," *"paq'qatát cilakátki"*

Denver Quarterly: "Resurrect," "Wintering / *he'elwéhtse*" (as "Wintering")

Drunken Boat: "This Dusk in a Mouth Full of Prayer"

Green Mountains Review: "You Are There, Almost, without a Name, without a Body, Go Now"

Gulf Coast: "Face-to-Face with One of the Gods," "*O. unilateralis s.l.*"

Hairstreak Butterfly Review: "This Faithful Purge, on Behalf of Your Heavenly Father"

Kenyon Review: "Self-Portrait as 1879–1934," "Self-Portrait toward a Fugue [No. ___ in ___♭ Minor]"

Massachusetts Review: "I Am Another of Yourself: Hand-Pounded Bark, Handmade Paper: Sumi Ink: Gayle Crites: 2016"

Mud City Journal: "Ant & Yellow Jacket"

Narrative: "Gather Up the Bones & Arrange Them Well," "On the Aggrieved," "On the Horizon," "A Soliloquy Would Imply That the Stage Is Empty"

PANK: "[Untitled]" (as "Prenatal")

Passages North: "Ligature," "Self-Portrait as Collected Bones [Rejoice Rejoice]"

Poetry: "A Poem for the *háawtnin'* & *héwlekipx* [the Holy Ghost of You, the Space & Thin Air]," "Portrait with Smeared Centuries"

Poetry Northwest: "Aposiopesis [or, The Field between the Living & the Dead]," "The Bones of Us"

Prairie Schooner: "A Boy & His Mother Play Dead at Dawn"

The Rumpus: "Swallowed Prayers as Creation" (as "These Swallowed Prayers as Creation Myth"), "Your Still-Life Is No Longer Still"

Winter Tangerine: "Testament #90," "World Made Visible"

"Aposiopesis [or, The Field between the Living & the Dead]," "I Say After-Rain, You Say *hahalxpáawisa*," "Self-Portrait as Article 1[1]. [Treaty with the Nez Percés, 1855]: Cession of Lands to the United States," "Self-Portrait as 1879–1934," and "This Dusk in a Mouth Full of Prayer" were included in the anthology *Native Voices: Indigenous American Poetry, Craft and Conversations* (Tupelo Press, 2019).

"Ant & Yellow Jacket," "A Boy & His Mother Play Dead at Dawn," "The Exile," "Gather Up the Bones & Arrange Them Well," "On the Aggrieved," "On the Horizon," "Resurrect," "Self-Portrait as Collected Bones [Rejoice Rejoice]," "Self-Portrait as 1879–1934," "Self-Portrait toward a Fugue [No. ___ in ___♭ Minor]," and "[Untitled]" (as "Prenatal") were translated by Béatrice Machet and included in the special French edition *Autoportrait aux siècles souillés* [Self-Portrait with Smeared Centuries] (Éditions des Lisières, 2018).

"Ant & Yellow Jacket," "The Exile," "On the Aggrieved," and "On the Horizon" were included in the chapbook *This American Ghost* (YesYes Books, 2017).

"Self-Portrait as 1879–1934" was included in *Best New Poets 2017* (University of Virginia Press, 2017).

"A Boy & His Mother Play Dead at Dawn" was included in *Bodies Built for Game: The Prairie Schooner Anthology of Contemporary Sports Writing* (University of Nebraska Press, 2019).

"The Exile" was included in the anthologies *Bettering American Poetry 2015* (Bettering Books, 2017) and *Imaniman: Poets Writing in the Anzaldúan Borderlands* (Aunt Lute Books, 2016), and was reprinted on the Academy of American Poets' website, Poets.org.

"Self-Portrait as Article 1[1]. [Treaty with the Nez Percés, 1855]: Cession of Lands to the United States" won the 2017 inaugural Adrienne Rich Award for Poetry from *Beloit Poetry Journal*, judged by Carolyn Forché.

"A Poem for the *háawtnin'* & *héwlekipx* [the Holy Ghost of You, the Space & Thin Air]" was included in *When the Light of the Sun Was Subdued, Our Songs Came Through: A Norton Anthology of Native Nations Poetry* (W.W. Norton, 2020).

•

I would like to offer *qe'ciyéw'yew'* to so many people who have helped me in not only the writing of this book but in making me and my work even possible:

To my *sepehitemenew'éet* who mentored me through guided breath, language, and stacks of pages. Kevin Goodan, Jen Richter, Claire Davis, Karen Holmberg, Beth Piatote, James Tarter, David Biespiel, Misty Urban, Chris Norden, Bessie Scott, *p'ínooc*, Harold Crook, Phillip Cash Cash, Haruo Aoki, Mary Lynn Walker, and Jim McCormack.

To *'inláwtiwaama* who gift me friendships across bodies of oceans and air, conversations, and the haven of sentences you turn into stories and poems and wisdom that continue to guide me to this day. Layli Long Soldier, Khaty Xiong, Sherwin Bitsui, Muriel Leung, Shangyang Fang, Ocean Vuong, Paul Tran, Eduardo C. Corral, Mari L'Esperance, Natalie Diaz, Leila Chatti, Elissa Washuta, Kazim Ali, Marco Wilkinson, Erika Wurth, Manny Loley, Jake Skeets, Byron Aspaas, Maggie Smith, Sarah Hennessey, Bessie *laymíwt* Blackeagle, Dominic Akkerman, Maeve Kirk, Sarah María Medina, Su Hwang, Billy-Ray Belcourt, Kaveh Akbar, Paige Lewis, Mariko Nagai, Afsheen Farhadi, Nick Goman, Jon Ross, Abbie Amabisca, Phillip Brown, Maya Polan, Nazifa Islam, Tomoko Minamizono, Shohei-kun, Kakeru Tanaka, Yoshi-san, Chie-chan, Tiki, and to Franny Choi, José Olivarez, Justin Phillip Reed, and Jane Huffman whose kindness welcomed me when I stepped back onto American soil for a few days in early October 2019.

To *temen'ew'éet* Béatrice Machet and to Maud Leroy of Éditions des Lisières who, countries and languages away, found me and believed fully in translating my voice across the borders of line-broken sentences.

To every indigenous writer, poet, and artist before and after me. You and the languages and worlds that make you are ever possible and limitlessly gorgeous.

To everyone at Copper Canyon Press who held these pages and said *yes, this one.* Especially to Michael, who never gave up on me and this book after health issues put my writing life in doubt, and to Elaina, who devoted so much time and care to editing this book with me.

To b: william bearhart who, years ago, messaged me and commented that the only press to which I should submit was the publisher that ultimately pressed this book into its spine and therefore its life. We all miss you eternal.

And to *nexce'éce kaa himyúume* who raised this shy, quiet boy with black hair over his eyes, who each taught me *wiiwyeteq'is* of being *nimíipuu*.

To *yáaca'* and *qánis* for surviving your lives with and into mine. To *na'yáac* Alexius for always sharing yourself with me, no matter what. To *piláqa'* who showed me, from my boyhood until I left the open door, our homelands by mountain, forest, river, season, and field.

To you *'iice'* who carried me into this world, despite everything that could have told you *no*. Every word I press to the page is an imprint of your survival.

na'íicyawa
for my mother

when it dawns for us
it is growing dark for you.

c'éewc'ew

CONTENTS

Aposiopesis [or, The Field between the Living & the Dead] | 5

I

Ezekiel 37:3 | 9

Swallowed Prayers as Creation | 11

Ant & Yellow Jacket | 13

Resurrect | 15

Testament #90 | 16

O. unilateralis s.l. | 18

Self-Portrait as 1879–1934 | 20

I Say After-Rain, You Say *hahalxpáawisa* | 22

Gather Up the Bones & Arrange Them Well | 23

Portrait with Smeared Centuries | 25

On the Horizon | 27

II

Objects in Mirror Are Closer Than They Appear | 31

A Boy & His Mother Play Dead at Dawn | 32

Wintering / *he'elwéhtse* | 34

Years Later, *ná'pláx,* in the Yard, Asks Me to Rename Him | 35

The Exile | 37

paq'qatát cilakátki | 41

Close to Each Other with [a/the] Body | 42

Self-Portrait as Collected Bones [Rejoice Rejoice] | 43

Ligature | 44

This Faithful Purge, on Behalf of Your Heavenly Father | 46

Self-Portrait as Article 1[1]. [Treaty with the Nez Percés, 1855]: Cession of Lands to the United States | 48

III

Face-to-Face with One of the Gods | 53

Your Still-Life Is No Longer Still | 55

A Poem for the *háawtnin'* & *héwlekipx* [the Holy Ghost of You, the Space & Thin Air] | 57

Self-Portrait toward a Fugue [No. ___ in ___♭ Minor] | 60

[Untitled] | 61

World Made Visible | 63

The Bones of Us | 65

This Dusk in a Mouth Full of Prayer | 69

A Soliloquy Would Imply That the Stage Is Empty | 71

On the Aggrieved | 76

I Am Another of Yourself: Hand-Pounded Bark, Handmade Paper: Sumi Ink: Gayle Crites: 2016 | 77

––––

You Are There, Almost, without a Name, without a Body, Go Now | 81

Notes | 85

About the Author | 89

SWALLOWED LIGHT

—

APOSIOPESIS [OR, THE FIELD BETWEEN THE LIVING &
THE DEAD]

& forgive me
for I cannot

tell you how
to begin

but here
is the body

like *the urge*
to pray—

your mouth
already gone.

& we never
said *you:* a boy

woman
man—only

the animal made
with two hands

& lost
in the field

waiting
for human life

to reenter
as if through

a door
broken—&

yet the dead
who love

you—who
are still

remembering
the touch

of blood-
warmed skin—

abandon you
like every

yesterday—
like this

single paradise
of every-

body's silence
rusting day-

light into
the only dusk

we have
been made

to see.

I

When I close my eyes I see / him, my lord. *Do you not
remember me?* I ask the half-buried / bones in ochre dust

& shedding / their deadened histories—*yóẋ yóẋ
yóẋ* they answer. Like a house / creaking open its doors

to reveal all that was left / behind. That day
what did I even know of a plea / but his beloved

body beginning to stir / against itself? My lord, here
is one shadow—our rainless valley / opening the earth

as though the entrance to a gun- / shot wound. Here
is where our graves echo / a nation & this nation

is yours / alone, my lord. It always was. / An oiled stroke
of forest smears the hills / days before the fire comes

to take us back. Here— / my lord, is the skull / joining
its spine—the body's standing / ladder—a column of rungs

like years of lives taken / & draped from the nape of the neck.
Lord, forgive me for I cannot / dance with you this way. As

these bones. As you leave / your imprint that the air eats
away like ghosts / the width of stories found

in translation. Where my heart is / the very same humming-
bird lifting the end / of every sunlit petal left / to be

shredded by any trace / of summer. Here, thirsted—
na'tóot I pronounce. & the dot appears / in his skull. It forms

just enough to fit this mouth- / swabbed bullet through / once
again—the way the North Star reenters / the skin

of every night—to salvage itself. & I can't / help but
turn away. For I'm afraid of the loss / of even my own

eyes. For I cannot bring myself / to peer into
those eyelets shaped in the image / of rain

puddles found / around the bodies of our nation. How they won't
stop boring into me. Like / this. & I just can't— / forgive

me, *tóota'*. With the lord / at my side as half of my skeleton
awaits your flesh—the forgotten half of me / to bloom back

over you like the start / of another hour. Ticking the sound
of jawbones desperate to swallow / the evening. Here, once

a field seared off tomorrow's / atlases. Once an ocean
of *qém'es* blooming out / of season—under the dead

light / draining the sky. *'íinim píst,* my lord, I see / his lips
as a kiss blown / apart—like the gift of first breath. / It's the blood-

rushing dark / rising from beneath his skin / beginning to flash
me back. *Soon this body / is yours to collect* you pledge

in their rattling tongue / of salvation. Here / is my father's
mouth / warmed—tightening / parted only by its weight—lord, look

into him. Like a well filled / with its unlit promise
toward water. & I promise to remember / this final opening

cocked back & waiting / to breathe. How this / singular fleshed jaw
is myself / now remade in its first shape. The body

before the body.

SWALLOWED PRAYERS AS CREATION

wáaqo' 'óykalana titóoqana hinéesmuxsin 'ilcwéew'cixnim.

Let me tell you a story: for ages, I have been holding on to our silence,
                a child learning to move his forsaken hands, to palm
      the walls of this godless place. I am
           your animal, a heart thrashing the air everywhere
& nowhere. Almost a torch—I reach for

        the entry to another room, this life-
            sized darkness like years fleshed around a skeleton. Listen:
the *xím xím xím* of the animals curls into *a body made to always be*
                      pinned by gravity &
             we have come

    so far, so let's disappear just this once
            into a land ready for our touch, the bloodstream around
      us carrying your body on & into the white noise
             of translation, the brief *sáw* between
        the ribs

hit by the oncoming light of our creation, a fresh fracture of a story throbbing
                like ear bones humming after
                 another heavy rain
          of gunfire: *now where were we going?* The myth insists
                  to pray

     for we might go back
          to when we were singing *láw láw láw* in our most gorgeous of
    animal skins, before the jaws of *'ilcwéew'cix* devoured us, before the cities
vanished into cathedrals
      of glittering bone,

& here,

        hear the dark—the whispers of the faceless drowning in
flesh triggered into motion. Oh, every exit a fire escape & nowhere

            to flee.

      The diaphragm above us doming

    like two skulls aching
to breathe. Listen for it: through the dead before us—our bodies inside
    this atrocious body—is the only way out, & the furred god
of this place says *run, you desperate*

      creatures. In this story: you run until your hind legs lift

           from the night sky
scraped onto the walls of this awful place, out beyond
     the smoke & ruin, until you are human enough,
  until the world is
    the world at last.

pamc'itpáaswisana, kawó' 'iceyéeyenm qepsqepsnéewitki
kaa hináashanya píswe.

támsoy kaa 'alatálo

Reach for

the slick hook

in my mouth:

bright hunger

a pulse between

us: & here

at the chest

a bee's heart

pressing an ant's

thorax before

collapsing. Who

said the body

would break

quite like this

that the face

could seal

another's? Feel

how alive

your skin is

how these lips

now lock yours:

when does

the breath finally

vanish as both

our bodies erupt

into a single arch

of basalt?

RESURRECT

náma kex kaa 'inciwáatx̣ kíne?

    'iceyéeye

    Or here—what's left of the living
room & warm light

    bulb hanging in the dark
        of our skulls. I only want you

    to know that once I turn off
the night, our shadows
        sleep stitched

    between us—one
is waiting to live again
    like a ghost wearing us

only when it wants—you—oh yes
    you will wake up by your-

    self in another room like rain
    retouching your lips with terrors

from the last century—begging the first question

    now: am I right to bring someone
anyone—
    back from the dead?

After today
you will be different: a god made soft

to never injure itself holds you facedown
to paradise: a myth is told at the end

of autumn when you are naked
with all the lights off & all you remember

is the voice of someone
you've forgotten: someone you said

you loved: so you stand here in the dark until
that song of flesh drowns your bones: & stays

like any starved god would: you are then asked
to build a fire: for the fallen snow

is already here in your blood: & you need
to run back through the pines: river swift

& curved into your calves: the limp limbs
of everyone you can no longer save

because you are but a boy: now gather the silent
wood & cut: know that this fire you build

will open its mouth when you want it
to live: to quench & eat: as January arrives

you are born in the cutout tongue of
winter: you are craving light: you crawl

from Father Above & toward the full-
bellied monster of His land & beg

to be spared.

O. UNILATERALIS S.L.

Dead ants were found under leaves, attached by their mandibles, on the northern side of saplings approximately 25 cm above the soil.

Sandra B. Andersen and others

You wear your bones outside

your skin / a lifetime of terror

in those ribs / you've been dancing

like a fox diving into hard snow

because *hunger* hums just there

beyond the body / you feel it

move through you like another

voice pressed to your bare throat /

now follow me the scented ghost

whispers between these trees

still clapping their hands / for you

are the bruised carpenter / my lord

building the last end of his life

as an undone bridge of dry bones

& *ququ ququ* like severed hooves

fastened to all these wetted arms

in the trees / your neck hanging

from invisible birds caught broken

in midflight / your mouth sealed

to the widest vein found / nearest

to what the body remembers

of those long winter skies / we are

forgiven / when we praise the ghosts

leaving their footprints to follow

in the forest / we think *summer*

burning among the frozen limbs

of these pines / *here* is *home*

& here you are / with every fire

cap & spore mushrooming through

you & that thorning head / I touch

after climbing the winded

aspen of this boyhood / an ant

smeared in a dab of sap / you

bored into a clay pot holding

a memory / your taste moving

across my slow-fruiting tongue.

It has darkened here only because the light is inside
the room. Now place your hand there. See. That—

no, this—this is your face & so: *what are you
but a citizen of this nation* you were born into

by no hands of your own. Like the architecture
of briefly lit churches, you stand here so silent

you're already another century broken
in two. Your mouth looks just like your father's

when he was living, weeping. Four white walls
in the dark. How his skin felt of scratched chalk-

board with each new written version of him
now so American: his name sparing his one blood-

red life. & see your mother kneeling at this quiet
cage of crushed windows that held the last image

of her black hair. Say you see nothing in this
language & everything inside *'intise pewiski, ne'é.*

ne'é? This tongue of animals you give to the starved
night. Like a lungful of gnashed syllables rusted

to the throat. Say *c'eewc'ew* like a promise made
of bone—because after the body, what's left

is bone. The jaw opened wide enough to say *your
name* like a wildfire spreading through your home-

land every summer when you are left to stand
in its pine forest. & god. The forest. Save me,

my lost savior. Save the boy who sees the blood
inside him. The forest. How it means: shadows

learning to breathe again—the disgraced light
here. It means all these branches are clotheslines

where nothing hangs anymore. It means you
touching the mirror is enough to crack apart

every America you've known since. It means no-
body is here. It means the ash in the dirt blown

to air was the braided hair of your ghosts longing
to welcome you back. Which is to say: yes, every-

one is here.

I call out to you like a / You whose flesh is cleared out / from our ghosted
shadows to the cracked lips of / the horizon. There you are / at the cathedral

in my mouth. A garden: *tamsáasnim láatis. líickaw. tíms* bloomed / in
dirt & scattered. The doorway. Are you honest enough to say / You've ever

loved? To not forget tearing / down every door to beat Your image / into
your son's memory? You know / a boy's name but do you know mine? Say

ixtab with a cord slung / around your neck. Say *cannibal. / 'ilcwéew'cix.* Or
tilípe' who leaps over / your deaths. Another dead / father is being brought

back to his son's thinning arms. / An ache that touches / the very wet end
of my tongue. Ignite me with this / blessing, Father. Give me this seventh

day to wash / You & your taste from my mouth. / Recall the ruined
entrance. The rust damaging / the architecture. Father, forgive me for / ever

asking. For a mother stands in your light / gone out. Screaming. Shattering
every last mirror in the house. To burn / the field & stand alone until the blood

of a forefather / rivers clean. Finally / motionless like the years / you've lived
You say: *the eighth day / I offer this eternal blessing.* Smelling of the dead

scorched grass: it starts to rain again.

GATHER UP THE BONES & ARRANGE THEM WELL

'óykalana pipísne 'ew'likítx ta'c

      'iceyéeye

Dawn again—
         & our sky gorges
               on everybody

stars discolored
             drowned in first light

honeyed
      & draining
          a wound—pressing gauze

across the mouthless face of night
             our dragged

feet an ankle's
       marrow rubbed
           into a milky way—

now gather each
      & every piece
            of your father

sing *náma kaa manáma*
         kaa mípx

hikúye hehéwlexne—
        to vanish from the skin

is this harvest of
      ruin lit
         in the mouth of a boy

behind the dimmed husk
                    of our eyelids

blots of auburn
                    this *sáw* after the rib cage wilts

after an autumn forgets it is
                    blinking winter a-

new blood running
                    our flowers fleshed—
                                        an opened vein
sunrises

PORTRAIT WITH SMEARED CENTURIES

I begin the day like any other
day: a decade staring back

in the rearview mirror
of the wrecked pickup truck: you

standing so tall you're already
headless: until I turn around

the cornfield blurs into the torn
edges of an atlas: pull your hands

out from under me to anoint
this god-gifted country of yours:

mottled bones singing
the anthem of a star-

spangled nation:
this land granted enough

time to list its own
possibilities: atrocities

a blade of dusk resting
on my throat, I bruise: by standing

I practice the sacred: & kneel
how the body was built

toward the bottomless insides
of ghosts: the small of my back

the sacrum: they say, the five
disciples with pocked faces,

not your self-inflicted gunshot
but a single entryway: an emptiness

full of faith: *rise to me* as only you
would after god has left

you with these entrance wounds
& no way out: the purpling field

that goes on & on: recognizable
as a heartbeat: a century-

long orbit around a cage
of stained glass: broken, you

gather me in your image
of failed flesh: piecing mirror

after mirror back together through
the night until no one forgets: one

hundred years of this landscape
behind & before us

continues to stir—even if
the earth under our knees,

under every American sky,
had been turning west-

ward for centuries.

ON THE HORIZON

& I said
let there be dark

pouring from between
the teeth. Let there be

an aftertaste in the back
of the throat. Let each locust

leap from the slow light
being dragged over the earth.

Let every angel not named
Michael ask *do you not know*

the single click in the mouth
is a tear you are

to always live in? Let the garden
remember *fire* for it is you

who will dress the wounds
of this place. Let lesser gods

forget you were ever born.
Let light begin &

black out from remembering
flesh as a touch to tell you

the skull once kissed the blood
laced with warmth

& held a body in place years ago.
That silence is forgotten

between each soft blow of the heart
until we finally stop. A name

we never speak anymore. A head
wound by living a life

here. Tonight let me tell you
the human form is meant to be

a beauty I will continue
to ruin.

II

Awake again, I find my name as
                          vanished as a midnight I want
      to salvage. To have those black teeth sinking back
                                into my skin—you enter me
through an opening in the sky
                  of my body like a face,
        a moon behind me falling slow
                      & moving its fingers to a mirror made
of the window above my bed. I hear the weight of its life
                          pressing down & the image
cracks. A figure stands
            in a gown of blued smoke—this *me*
                    & *you*—a shadow laid over
        the surface of a puddle. Its eyes
                  lit up like those
of wolves brimming with winter. So let this body. Let it go:
                  as though a breath
      wanted to be saved, I part my mouth into
                púuceyxceyxne & *into pieces*
as I am. But language between the lips
                 shrapneled into air is all that ever touches
      the never-seen
pink of my lungs. I breathe in & breathe out. For what
               we've lost—my dear
ghosts. The sound of the field
      long after the war

A BOY & HIS MOTHER PLAY DEAD AT DAWN

*The presence of mothers and babies in the blue
rifle smoke that made dawn more dim.*

C.E.S. Wood, 1884

Tucked beneath
    a bank of brush.
Held between my legs
    are my hands.
Like prayer.
    Like holding in
my morning piss.
    & I do. It's warmer
at the lip's edge
    of pinked water. Is it
the dead we're about
    to become?
She dunks me
    beneath. Purpled
ripples erasing me.
    Some hunched men
check the grounds
    for skulls. Some
will drag the dead us
    to the open mouth
of the creek. & of
    course they smell
me. She nods:
    cepée'yehey'ckse
I'll make you
    soft by soaking,
my son when she floods
    around me. I pull in

my tongue from any
        taste. We flower
from the inside out.
        Please don't mistake
her for another now.
        I'm still. Dawn
mirrored then crushed
        by another hidden rain
of hollowed gunmetal.
        This slow-motion
massacre crowding
        silenced. Each body
pressing her freed weight
        into me. Mouth
agape. *tequúse 'iin. This*
        warmth. Drown
me I beg no one. Hurry.
        Empty me out.

Bones scatter toward paradise, & the boy is kept until day
        breaks. How like mothers we are told to always love beyond
                        our broken hands. Silhouettes
emerge along the road & perch as near
                    as the early song sparrows bursting
            to air. When we touch the bodied remains of that world,
history is a fist shivering in the warmth
                    of a gasping mouth, & tomorrow is then
today. The boy
        who once bathed in the crushing between two
                        bodies of cleaned water
reaches from
        lifted dark & into the first throb
                            dawn makes when we forget
            how even the hours kiss the singed lips
of deserted angels. *Someone left alive,* whose skin chirps like a belly-
                ful of crickets, whispers *'aqáamkin'ikaay* once
            because the boy
is built to be—as if a savior's first
                budding season—the very same light that thaws
        the snowflakes strung through this countried air. It's winter
here, remember: *he'élwehtse* remains so
                        written on his skin, & tell him, when he is
        found, O please—to scour our bones when hungered,
                                when human.

YEARS LATER, *NA'PLÁX̣*, IN THE YARD, ASKS ME TO
RENAME HIM

At the foot of
    this mountain you

are the boy alone
    again: there is

a word rusted
    to the back of

your throat: a deer
    shed what was

burning: velvet-
    tipped building

of its own bones
    gnarled from

its soft head: you
    find it warmed

near a trunk with
    long neck-wound

shapes scratched
    into wet pine bark

like how our names
    looked before

being so tongued
    by America: &

that gleaming
    double helix of

your dried uvula
    blackens to

ash: your grandson
    will greet you

tonight: you'll weep—
    praying: word

for word in
    a sound like

a beggar plucked
    of his teeth.

THE EXILE

Chilocco Indian School, Oklahoma, 1922: A disciplinarian says, *There is no foolishness, do everything just so . . . such as keep your room clean, keep yourself clean, and no speaking of your Native language.*

Titus Paul

For now I can
            just whisper
kál'a sáw

                        the *'óxoxox*
    of my *hím' k'up'íp*

wrecked at the base
                of a century that burns

through my slow blood

                    •

                        kiké't caught

in the blink   *silúupe*

so draw the eyelids
        shut & forget the fire
tangled among the branches

of your spine
            start where the skin meets

half an autumn
        rusting the edge of winter that is

37

knifing   between me & *'iin*

you & *'iim 'ee*

                            •

        boy   *have you forgotten us*

                                    is not what they are saying

or are they   asks another century

                how are we remembered
        in our choreography
of bones?

                            •

mouth your birthplace   boy
without mouthing off   *tim'néepe*   is *at the heart*

or *the heart of the monster*

                    or *the grass blood-soaked*

from the fresh kill that finally isn't

                            your father

& pray *héwlekce* when your body is given away   says the orphan boy

                with lashes licked into his shoulders

forget *'im'íic*   because they can   tear every lip from every memory

of your mother

•

because you are
torn & because you are
what song fills
   your throat
with the color
   of carved-out tongue

peewsnúut & *hi'lakáa'awksa*
   is what you only hear in the dark
& so what does it mean
                    asks the boy—

•

as the moon
glows jaws wide
to the unbearable
taste of ash
blown among the stars

that the boy learned
the ghost's trail

that *milky way*
is lit by the dying
brightly echoed

•

c'ewc'éewnim 'iskit
so there had to be breathing

there had to be.

PAQ'QATÁT CILAKÁTKI

'ilx̱líiwe-

        céew cew-

céew hiwsiix, ne'é

        'iink'e cíiq'ce:

paq'qatát hipew'-

        céeye, 'itúune

'ewéwluqse: him'

        hin'ipéecwise

sáw

        sáw yóx̱-

óx̱ox̱

        'ícicici-

ca'ya 'enesmiss-

        ukíse: hin'éeptin'ix

'imím ciláakt

        hím'ki tíim'enin—

CLOSE TO EACH OTHER WITH [A/THE] BODY

(half whisper / half ghost)

                        (second half of the ghost[s] &

a stressed whisper) there are these (ghosts / whispers) about, aren't there?

                    I (too) want word-movement (to speak):

close (to each other) they—

                    came (closer), what (thing)

do you want: a mouth

                    I desire (to speak into motion)

(silence / lone body / desperate / lonely)

                    (silence [yet sound] that there [yet bones

hitting against each other])

                    (the mouth / body [whose?] shivers)

(nothing) by sound

                    I recognize (them): they are holding (yet holding a *wake* for)

your body

                    with/by the mouth—(it / you) is / are (in the state of being) written—

SELF-PORTRAIT AS COLLECTED BONES [REJOICE REJOICE]

after Paris auction of indigenous human remains & objects

For there's a polished-bright medal
of honor hanging in my chest like another
man's stilled heart: for I lie here
waiting for you in fields
broken by hands the same shapes as
howitzer blasts: for I am
learning to stand up again
with only cleaned bones: singing *rejoice*
rejoice are the quieted rib cages of our beloved
nation: for the massacre is only
a series of colorless photographs, archives
of snow & nothing else: Mother, tell me
what you remember of another man's hand
reaching into your throat
like a night-frozen glove: how warm
was it? Was it him with the words
of a god beaded over his lips like sweat? For
the wounded is someone touched
& entered with the weapon we shape
into fingerprints: no matter how wrecked
or soft: we return to the field
wrapped in this one name
under god: *rejoice rejoice,* say the hand-
bones that want the heft of memory:
for I am a decade: a century
of openmouthed thirst
even as the snow keeps falling—
& falling through:

LIGATURE

after Eduardo C. Corral

I swing
     from a rope
          lashed

to a beam. Is it
     the dead
          who are afraid

of recalling
     prayer? Wasn't it:
          browned wrists

bared knees
     a sweat-slick neck
          even the small

of the back
     that corrects me
          into worship?

Don't tell me
     what I've seen.
          Please don't. Look

beyond my eyes.
     There's so much
          I wanted

to say
     before the body:
          attempted flight.

To swing
      & lash
            to beam

before the lord
      breaks the ghost
                  free

from the curve
      of the spine—
            to surrender

to the trees'
      bright ovation
          like a steady fall

of sweet rain
          on the field.

THIS FAITHFUL PURGE, ON BEHALF OF YOUR HEAVENLY
FATHER

Watch as a war twists from my teeth, from the tongue
                                        crushed between

the desperation of my parted lips, the first entrance
                                        to my throat. A first kiss

tells you everything. Spare me
                                        the soft agony of living

another daybreak as it's swallowed
                                        by night. I walk to the field's

center. Sagebrush smeared
                                        by distance. Alfalfa around my ankles.

& I open
                                        my palms. I lie down here to face you. Cut off

my hair. Undress. I'm naked
                                        for you. I ready my shining skull so

soon to be slick. Revealing
                                        gashes the color of

swollen eyes.
                                        My body holds its own blood-

washed scalp, as if a prayer
                                        ached to be this real, as if every word

I lose is a newer sky teaching me this
                                        is already more than a body

could ever handle. Now I take my hair,

                half a life's worth of dark & length,

& light my father's

                orange BIC lighter. Because I raze

the field & have for centuries,

                my mouth to revere. For what's left

in ash is the shape of a boy

                like the exiled beast who kneels

before the fire &—without another

                sound—disappears.

SELF-PORTRAIT AS ARTICLE 1[1]. [TREATY WITH THE NEZ PERCÉS, 1855]: CESSION OF LANDS TO THE UNITED STATES

In the year of their lord, *this eleventh day of June,* I enter the boundaries of my body:

The said [centuries here dissolve & I re-ink *nimíipuu*] hereby cede, relinquish & convey—here,

I want to convey how my physical testament is written &, at a particular point, then erased into the land—

to the United States all their right, title & interest in & to the country occupied or claimed by them,

bounded & described as follows, to wit:

in the year of their lord, in the boundaries of my body, *they* intend to clarify the divisions & say *to wit:*

& so I enter every name of the dead into each source of water, each river mouth, every flattened field:

& I cross out the cross of the divide & lie down on the crest of [every mountain has its name,

a place of, a place of where the animals & humans met, a place where the story began, a place where the blood was washed, a place at the heart named for our monster(s) & tim̓néepe,

a place where the gray coldness looms like hiqúsqúxcenki, where America names over the land (lapclápc

wéetes), a place where the blue haze of warmth looms like hi'lap'ápx̌p'apx̌canki, where the bodies lie

unburied]. I, a silhouette, a hereunto, am between the articles of the & a(n): definite, indefinite:

& it is here in the boundaries I have no choice but: to set [my] hands, on this eleventh day of June,

on behalf of the abovenamed, at the place, on the day & year hereinbefore written, to seize the body

shut:

•

[x] [an empty cross, fallen]

Sealed & signed in the presence of us—

49

III

FACE-TO-FACE WITH ONE OF THE GODS

'éetu: so be it, he says—
& I ignite a flame

striking a wooden match
along the torso of

my god: a face mirroring
a boy afraid of only him-

self: a shadow
spills behind us

like long-standing firs
on the first broken

morning of the new year:
he slides a finger inside

my mouth: a forgotten bird-
song droning louder than

our shivering: my tongue
I feel bruising: his fingertip

somehow a softened pit
of fruit: this sugared

nail: my mouth shut
as I look up to him

in the light: wind
through the trees: wind in

his matted fur: my hair
a forest fire: our faces now

gone—but the taste
of one last chance

to swallow.

YOUR STILL-LIFE IS NO LONGER STILL

Your hands bright red as the skin / of the Red Delicious

we shredded / to taste what's closest / to the core / this

isn't the blood / of our newest ghosts / the snow

touching the skin / of only the living / will become

beads / of breakable sky / shiver, my dear— / for we are

soon to be so / gone / this same land is smearing / into

America / my hair smelling / of river water—is this

an omen? a telling? a foreshadow? now tell me / we'll make it

to the end / of our impossible lives / tell me how / the cities

will make our bodies / beautiful enough to forever / be locked

behind a glass cage / with our broken names / teach my tongue

the only way / to dance until the whorl / of dark silk below

your belly- / button is as slick as the pink / of our animal

tongues / give me / the directions to a place / bursting with

mosquitoes—full of / welts & terrors you'll always know / we'll know

the coming / of someone's jesus let's call *hunger* / dear,

it's the end / of winter so / sleep next to me until / the black

under our eyelids / is no longer the thinnest slip of skin

but the mid- / night of a country growing / before us

tell me this / will never ruin us / god, tell me / please.

A POEM FOR THE *HÁAWTNIN'* & *HÉWLEKIPX* [THE HOLY GHOST OF YOU, THE SPACE & THIN AIR]

'inept'ipéecwise ciláakt: (I am wanting to) hold a wake /
(I am wanting to) hold the body

Had this body been made
                    of nothing

but its bright skeleton & autumn-

blown skin
            I would shut my eyes

into butterfly wings
        on a mapped earth. Had the gods

even their own gods, I could re-

learn the very shape
            of my face in a puddle of sky-

colored rain. Extinction is
                    to the hands

as the lips are
            to the first gesture

the tongue carves into the slick mouth

just before
            prayer. In every way

the world fails
            to light the soft inner

57

machine & marrow

     of the bones in motion—I imagine

smudging my tongue along a wall
                           like the chest

I dare to plunge in-
       to, the braille of every node

blooming out
              as if the first day-

light of wintered
             snowfall. This night—

like any fleshed boy I dream
               of a lyre strung

with the torn hair of *hímiin* &
                 in place

of my dried mouth—there
               it is. Whispers

in the blue-black dark after *c'álalal*

c'álalal reach out
           toward my teeth to strum

this wilting instrument. &
            once awake, I'm holding

its frame to build
           a window back in-

to the world. Had this body

been held after all

        these years, I would enter

you to find my frozen self

& touch. Like the gutted animal

                we take

in offering. & live.

Even in my wildest dreams, there I am
held in the arms of my country: a country leaving
me with the crushed shine of a man's shadow: where I am
a boy again surrounded by my god's
failure of a forest: where the bodies of men are
silhouettes slipping their fingers
down my throat: I say I will change the world
in my wildest dreams—which means the bullets loaded
in my mouth are only teeth: & only crooked teeth
& not the white lilac-
like stains leading me to a window: so clear
in my wildest dreams, my hands are like this:
gone—fingerprints the braille of a mouth
reading *touch* & moving like sound emptied
into a perfectly rounded hole: in my wildest dreams
I forget the colors left behind
my eyelids: & the blinking of every eye-
witness—the murderers held so close
I swear they're in my hands: in the window
my skin is turned to
a human-hollowed doorway—I shatter
what *light* has done to me: in my wildest dreams
where the given body is a form of flight
& in this latest version I step into
the wreckage—to find the other side of
me blooming toward *you.*

[UNTITLED]

But before you live
you must remember every word
your mother never said.
As in here's the most perfect hole
to reach into
because what remains
is a space like the hands
you're beginning
to forget. Promise me
before you live
you'll remember the darkest
you'll have ever been
won't be holding steady
a cocked barrel in your mouth
the wheat field below the house lit
by another autumn. It was always me blooming
you inside me. Before living
swear to me you'll forget
the way a body carves out its own
season to lie down in.
To never forget the trees
lining the field before the sun
sets at last. Beyond are the torn ghosts
you are to always remember.
There is a voice that leaves
will always hold for you there.
& before you live
you must remember that night
is always falling somewhere
in the world. Someday autumn
could be just another hole
that winter empties into.

Remember me for this hunger
I brought you into. That your warm
body has never lived
without me.

& this is where you stand with a gun the size of American centuries that has already entered your boyish body but in this version of the lullaby the gun isn't loaded with bullets but the teeth of those who sang you your first name it sounded like bones rattling against one another in the back of your throat until you could finally say x̌ayx̌áy̌x̌ like the once-silvered color of a standing skeleton against the backdrop of a sky-sized moon holding itself together with pins that look nothing like rusted barbs but bird beaks desperate to open & call out to the thinning air to please *please* take us back to the paradise where we learned to breathe again to *let me breathe* with the sound of every child running down streets made in the age of another war held to itself like a suicide in the closet of your best friend who said *let me tell you everything everything will be better don't worry I'll see you tomorrow* & what she meant was *I'm not planning on coming back but I do I do love you enough to be the last person I see* & that means your body is enough to carry the image of her & looking in the mirror & letting the world decide what to do with the body when we must first carry her to the mountain you call *home* & calling out her name to the wind moving through the pine branches like wind chimes that hold your voice in their grip & crumble it along the dirt road like facedown breath kicked from the ceremony of your mouth & someday the sunlight will kiss you once & turn as black as your shadow along the wall of your father's prison cell before he killed another man with his bare hands because *anyone can kill a man but I can do it better* so you never saw him until you cut your finger along the shining body of a knife he gave you to keep under your bed for the nightmares are coming *they're coming be ready for every nightmare be a man ain't no goddamn dream catcher gonna do shit for you & so here're some shrooms too boy* & you know the color of your blood is the same color of a murderer who only wanted to live as another human & that's what it means when we are told to enter the story spoken in the language your ghosts still talk to you in we hear the voice enter the body like a swallowed sword how it scrapes the vertebrae surrounding your spine that you can snap into a makeshift ladder to another lifetime & you're alone again aren't you you're alone at the edge of an ocean that never asked you to come & there is an orange tree that stands naked & never cries until you turn your back & walk toward the one-eyed moon that hides its wrecked face like another god

calling *your name* but never once your family name because it remains illegible
& too forgotten to recall like the palm on your chest when you ask *where's the*
mystery in the light & the voice inside your head is answering *it's the dark* & you'll
never find it unless you close your eyes now & remember how you came this far
without losing yourself to another war on your American body another war on
your ghostlike skin another war holding itself to the horizon-colored window
of your room when everyone whom you love is only farther away the longer
you breathe & tonight when you dream you plan on never breathing again but
someone saying something like *manáa wees?* means you're unsure whether the
dream knows you're never coming back this far again until every light in the world
turns off for one solid minute you find inside a bottle with a small animal inside
whispering to you *I came looking for you & found myself* shipwrecked on this island
of erased butterflies & unopened jawbones & you know the animal's name in
your grandfather's language that was beaten from him & you say *I'm Telemachus*
it's so nice to meet you again, Father but you're only lying enough to feel the heat on
your back from a city imagined & meant to be burning so you wake up on a boat
in the dock of the port with everyone in the village asleep until morning & you've
been crying the whole night with a gun there & a tooth-sized bullet with a note
that reads *love—your Father 'iinim pist* is nothing like saying *Daddy* or *darling*
darling hold me here because it's night & this singular ocean isn't going anywhere
only you are only you are going somewhere as far as your body will let you so ask
your shadow anything & remember *don't worry don't worry you're not going to die*
I promise I swear the night always falls & that this is the end of everything unless
you remember that the salt water is only as black as the inside of your eyelids &
this is where you stand with the gun the size of centuries & now take it from your
spent mouth & enter the warmth of the water where you were once made of too
many midnights running under a terrified American sky & now you—you who
believed that *everything changes despite the loss of light*—now you're made to make
your body blood-gorgeous again.

THE BONES OF US

I could mistake a life for
                              too many dusks darkening
               along the spine. Somebody was saying

the skeleton of our faith, *the skeleton of our faith*

                              but whose? There are two-

          hundred & six bones that hold
                    the human body like this: ninety-four

bones have disappeared from you. So forgive me—

                              no. They are always still
          there inside you. Rejoicing how they
                    merged into this *you*. Rejoicing

like a day's worth of light hitting your body
          fleshed with only its rib cage. A mother was said

     to shoot back at the cavalry—for crushing
               her baby's head. It was dawn. So many of us, so
why remember it now?

                    The first time I went to church I cried

in that Sunday school closet. A boy said *Jesus won't save you*
                              after you die. My body only
     walled off by skin. These borders my ghosts agreed on.

                              Somewhere between
          my jawline & throat
                    is an animal-
               skinned god left out for good.
     Counting back down to zero.

65

                       & when the lamps are left on in the house
the first sound I lose

                                   is the forest
             dressed in fire.

Every summer was this: fields & fields
                      of ash. Someone said
           it's like midnight scraped from a muffler. & I believed

       I was awake
                in the ochre-blasted wheat: talking &

talking bones. Back & forth. A rust-on-rust kind of conversation
                         about every story

carved into the land like a numbered testament on the inside
                     of the mouth.

      My mother spoke at night about hunger like a child
                     holding together the face
           of his first art project. Of course

it was in her likeness: the yarn
            her hair. But what she meant was
                every day is an act of starvation.

     & I promised my body to so many. But my living body was
                        in a way
        already spoken for. So I stopped.

I stopped & put my ear to your belly. You said, *listen for the aurora*

in your own lungs.

                   Now when living is a season
across a field, what's between us breathing
           & the dead left staring back is our savior

motioning *the ghost reached down*
                    & then brought his hand to his mouth.

         He was told: be obedient.
                              Like any decent animal. Placing
invisible serviceberries on his tongue & eating
                              into a stillness
     an air unfinished for far too many reasons.

& darling, if our mouths ever happen
                    to touch: remember—
     it means only that I am speaking
                    inside you. That we have always been
          speaking to each other.

Why: a man with a single tongue asks about our survival
                    & means extinction? The softness of the body
          is not the flesh: but the footprints

     of the gods who once lived there—& abandoned their homes to us.

                         This bruised air, the promised land
of angels lying facedown
                    in the grass with no memory
          of who had left them there
     for dead.

I could mistake this year for any other
                    grave I've dug. For someone

     saying *boy, welcome to your life.* I didn't know that

the hands were nothing
                              but chapels—
     were everything we said
                    they could be—a shadow of the faces

you always wanted to hold

                     back. I look into a mirror, afraid.

Afraid to whisper: *look at yourself before you enter another*

                           life today. I stare like the last mirror
I remember breaking.

When you first came
                    into my mouth
            opened wide enough

to forget
                    how to swallow

light: this surrendering

                    the body is my skin

tracing starved beauty
                    in climax: *us*

lying in the dark
                    shadow of another
        lord: give me your dying

words like *father*

                    or *my tongue*

disappearing before
                    you: welik'ipckse
so tell me this

when you've forgotten
                    how to open

your lips into my name—

                    father: which is
another way to say *shadow:*

failed daylight
                    you say: *the sky*

touching the body: I
      find myself entering

a night again wounded
      enough for the snow—

shined with moon
      —to reorder the stars with
our faces: broken

      through with so many

American mouths: like
            ghosts singing

the very last bright word they

remember: *amen.*

A SOLILOQUY WOULD IMPLY THAT THE STAGE IS EMPTY

The body was found
    haloed by flies—& I looked beautiful

in their thousands of eyes.
        Didn't I? Tell me

how every eye
         is more than a window
    into a childhood's October-

red heaven. I write my name
backward for you

        to read my body
in your own
      forsaken reflection.

•

I came to—to the sound of a river
breaking through my front door. The wall: *as white as*
god's unbroken bones: the silence written there
until I turned off the lights. The water was rising
to my lips. I held my breath, forgetting how
to cave the last eyehole to earth. So I shut my eyes
& breathed—tasting the blue of dawn
flooding my lungs. The sky
was quiet.

•

The sharp key of F ringing the air / I promise I'm not / hearing things, I beg /
for another master / to smash my jaw into the color of my eye- / lids, their all-
day dark before surrendering to their own / breaking blood vessels & / this is the
way it was / always supposed to be: / my master yawning / the land behind us
dissolving—

•

Tell me why daylight only swells when the dark fails to bloom:

Open your mouth & let me in, some (body's) god whispered down my spine.

•

A father broke / the table. A father cracked / the orbital bone in a language I
only know / now: today. A father peeled the night / from another midnight &
begged / me to lie / still. Years later, in the yard, under hours of moonlight, I
broke down / & ran through the summer wheat: I disappeared / for weeks. I
drowned / a father in the river / promising him / I'd stay / alive.

•

Don't tell me how
         this ends, dear. You're already

licking the end
         of a black metal barrel like

the fingertip of someone
         you are failing

to love.

                              •

It was years ago I found his hands by playing shadow puppets during a blackout.
He flashed once against the window & revealed the same face: mine.

The body needs its vertebrae to curve. To lock itself into his black guitar case in
the basement pantry. To never return. I opened it like a door to another century.
Nothing grows there anymore.

I pulled a strand of hair & watched it turn into a centipede. A snake. An amputated
arm. Phantom limb. My palms dusted in ash. I licked the lines of my open hand
until they curled into smoke.

                              •

I'm gone like everyone else.

I'm building a bed for every-

one. At this rate—like thirst

I may never finish.

•

Where are you, *tóota*?

                 [the sky was never there in the first place]

Lord, why divide this land—this body?

                 [the ceiling / a hard thud / the red
                 of a war / inside someone's head]

•

& instead, as in the hunger
             sinking inside
    every ghost I've craved
to remember, I'm
            kneeling—praying

for this sinner to be
            saved. Heaven answers back:

Go. Save yourself. Run
    until *running* is no longer

a word your mouth can ever
                        shape again.

Carve the wind apart
                into one single
lasting answer. Find the body
                        there—

under its exile. Its ruin
                of spent vowels.

There's a white wall & just beyond
is another—a soft voice says just behind
me. Every friend you've ever had will pass
through here. The kitchen is a mess.
Isn't it your turn to wash the dishes again?
Go make kindling for this wall. The hatchet's there.
Warm up this house because it's winter again
& *skin* is another word for forgetting your blood
is in motion. Check the closet where your brother is held
four inches above the carpet. Take his large hands
to clean the ash in the fire stove. Check the dresser
for the pistol your mother gave your nephew.
Search the pillows for any resin left
of every dream here whittled down by another beginning
to night. We call that *dusk*. So get naked & turn off
the light you've left on for twenty-five years. Silly boy. Look
in the mirror. When you hold his left-handed knife to the thick
vein in your neck do you hear the wall say *steady
yourself*? Or is it *him'pe'ewytin hiwc'éeye* because it's better
to shoot yourself in the mouth? To hear a name call
back to you through a silence made from
a body half yours. Take the buck knife & finally cut
into the paint. Part what you can. Until it's nothing
but you & every broken-open body standing together
in the room. Put your hand through
the hole you made. Reach out to the unspoken
rainfall cooling your wrecked hands. Say to it that
there's a white wall. Say you broke past the bones & into
the heart. Reach farther until you touch another
hand & you know someone's there just outside. Feel
how the rain might slow into snow & your breath
brightens from the dark held in your mouth.

I speak to
this made flesh
like *latitláatit*
hilatíyo the gun-
hole opens
its one eye
& once I woke
up in a room
holding the skull
of *niséeweynu*
only my father
killed where I
then skinned it
that morning
with only one
arm my right
arm was out
to gather all of
this world like
fallen branches
for a fire &
afterward I
held the gun-
shot in my
head as long
as I could
until the air
stopped &
every nerve
in the body
whispered to

me like *kix*
wapa'áyks so
I did I swear
I washed
the blood
from my
hands & let
my last
eye open.

—

YOU ARE THERE, ALMOST, WITHOUT A NAME, WITHOUT A BODY, GO NOW

You find the house
burning again & every-

one inside: the plum
trees, skeletal

in the backyard
like an entrance

to every secret we have
ever mouthed: how

our teeth left intact, after
centuries, were our own

little blessings—even
for every daylit lashing

we had to take: for your
tongue: open the door

to find another *you*
talking to your mother

in a newer language so
American you've longed

just to remember: your
father—it is said somewhere

in a leather-bound book
of translations you've torn

from its rotted spine—can
only be here as long

as he carries
what remains of

the back of his hand-
warmed head. &

he's here, isn't he—
with the very same

smile as god's
final bullet retracing

its arc from
a faint line of black

shadow: *come here, you*
without a body—

my nameless baby
boy: before the house

collapses in-
to the horizon's

monstrous throat: come
here, my dear,

& tell me every story
about the directions

you found in your
own lungs—about

breathing to find
your way home.

Both the book's epigraph and "Aposiopesis [or, The Field between the Living & the Dead]" allude to "Coyote and the Shadow People," a Nez Percé tale that is akin to the Greek myth "Orpheus and Eurydice."

"Self-Portrait as 1879–1934" is for and after Beth Piatote and her book *Domestic Subjects: Gender, Citizenship, and Law in Native American Literature.*

"Ligature" borrows the lines "I swing from a rope / lashed / to a beam" from "All the Trees of the Field Shall Clap Their Hands" by Eduardo C. Corral.

"Self-Portrait as Article 1[1]. [Treaty with the Nez Percés, 1855]: Cession of Lands to the United States" reuses legal language from the Treaty of Walla Walla, 1855, specifically articles 1 and 11.

"[Untitled]" is for and always after my mother.

"The Bones of Us" was sparked from Natalie Diaz's prose poem "The Hand Has Twenty-Seven Bones" and includes the line "the ghost reached down and then brought his hand to his mouth" from the Nez Percé story "Coyote and the Shadow People."

"On the Aggrieved" was written after a poetry prompt by Heather Brown during a graduate student and alumni group project called Project Poetry, an idea created and spearheaded by Phillip Watts Brown. The poem also borrows the traditional name *him'pe'ewyíin* (Shot-in-the-mouth).

"*I Am Another of Yourself:* Hand-Pounded Bark, Handmade Paper: Sumi Ink: Gayle Crites: 2016" includes the word *niséeweynu,* the special term for Coyote. The typical word for coyote/Coyote is *'iceyéeye.* My teacher Harold Crook and our elders note the special heft of this word when in context.

"You Are There, Almost, without a Name, without a Body, Go Now" uses as its title the fifth line of the poem "Five Directions to My House" by Juan Felipe Herrera.

The majority of the *nimipuutímt* language used throughout this book comes from personal written notes, elders and teachers, memories, stories, and the paramount language work of Haruo Aoki's *Nez Perce Dictionary* and Archie Phinney's *Nez Percé Texts.*

ABOUT THE AUTHOR

Michael Wasson is a 2018 Native Arts & Cultures Foundation National Artist Fellow in Literature and a 2019 Ruth Lilly & Dorothy Sargent Rosenberg Poetry Fellow. He is from the Nez Percé Reservation in Idaho.

Lannan Literary Selections

For two decades Lannan Foundation has supported the publication and distribution of exceptional literary works. Copper Canyon Press gratefully acknowledges their support.

LANNAN LITERARY SELECTIONS 2022

Chris Abani, *Smoking the Bible*

Victoria Chang, *The Trees Witness Everything*

Nicholas Goodly, *Black Swim*

Dana Levin, *Now Do You Know Where You Are*

Michael Wasson, *Swallowed Light*

RECENT LANNAN LITERARY SELECTIONS FROM COPPER CANYON PRESS

Mark Bibbins, *13th Balloon*

Sherwin Bitsui, *Dissolve*

Jericho Brown, *The Tradition*

Victoria Chang, *Obit*

Leila Chatti, *Deluge*

Shangyang Fang, *Burying the Mountain*

June Jordan, *The Essential June Jordan*

Laura Kasischke, *Lightning Falls in Love*

Deborah Landau, *Soft Targets*

Rachel McKibbens, *blud*

Philip Metres, *Shrapnel Maps*

Aimee Nezhukumatathil, *Oceanic*

Paisley Rekdal, *Nightingale*

Natalie Scenters-Zapico, *Lima :: Limón*

Natalie Shapero, *Popular Longing*

Frank Stanford, *What About This: Collected Poems of Frank Stanford*

Arthur Sze, *The Glass Constellation: New and Collected Poems*

Fernando Valverde, *America* (translated by Carolyn Forché)

Matthew Zapruder, *Father's Day*

Poetry is vital to language and living. Since 1972, Copper Canyon Press has published extraordinary poetry from around the world to engage the imaginations and intellects of readers, writers, booksellers, librarians, teachers, students, and donors.

COPPER CANYON PRESS WISHES TO EXTEND A SPECIAL THANKS
TO THE FOLLOWING SUPPORTERS WHO PROVIDED FUNDING
DURING THE COVID-19 PANDEMIC:

4Culture
Academy of American Poets (Literary Relief Fund)
City of Seattle Office of Arts & Culture
Community of Literary Magazines and Presses (Literary Relief Fund)
Economic Development Council of Jefferson County
National Book Foundation (Literary Relief Fund)
Poetry Foundation
U.S. Department of the Treasury Payroll Protection Program

WE ARE GRATEFUL FOR THE MAJOR SUPPORT

PROVIDED BY:

TO LEARN MORE ABOUT UNDERWRITING
COPPER CANYON PRESS TITLES,
PLEASE CALL 360-385-4925 EXT. 103

WE ARE GRATEFUL FOR THE MAJOR SUPPORT
PROVIDED BY:

Richard Andrews
Anonymous (3)
Jill Baker and Jeffrey Bishop
Anne and Geoffrey Barker
In honor of Ida Bauer, Betsy
  Gifford, and Beverly Sachar
Donna Bellew
Matthew Bellew
Sarah Bird
Will Blythe
John Branch
Diana Broze
John R. Cahill
Sarah Cavanaugh
Stephanie Ellis-Smith and
  Douglas Smith
Austin Evans
Saramel Evans
Mimi Gardner Gates
Gull Industries Inc. on behalf of
  William True
The Trust of Warren A. Gummow
William R. Hearst III
Carolyn and Robert Hedin
David and Jane Hibbard
Bruce Kahn
Phil Kovacevich and Eric Wechsler

Lakeside Industries Inc. on behalf
  of Jeanne Marie Lee
Maureen Lee and Mark Busto
Peter Lewis and Johnna Turiano
Ellie Mathews and Carl Youngmann
  as The North Press
Larry Mawby and Lois Bahle
Hank and Liesel Meijer
Jack Nicholson
Gregg Orr
Petunia Charitable Fund and
  adviser Elizabeth Hebert
Suzanne Rapp and Mark Hamilton
Adam and Lynn Rauch
Emily and Dan Raymond
Joseph C. Roberts
Jill and Bill Ruckelshaus
Cynthia Sears
Kim and Jeff Seely
Joan F. Woods
Barbara and Charles Wright
In honor of C.D. Wright,
  from Forrest Gander
Caleb Young as C. Young Creative
The dedicated interns and
  faithful volunteers of
  Copper Canyon Press

The Chinese character for poetry is made up of two parts:
"word" and "temple." It also serves as pressmark for
Copper Canyon Press.

The poems are set in Adobe Garamond Pro.
Book design and composition by Phil Kovacevich.